NOT HIM OR HER

Accepting and Loving My Non Binary Child

Here's what you should know

Michelle Mann

CONTENTS

INTRODUCTION

So, your child has identified as non-binary. What does that mean for you as a family? How do you deal with their declaration? Is it just a phase they are going through? Are they ill? And how on earth are you going to tell the rest of your family and friends?

All of those questions and more are answered in this guide for parents whose child has come out as non-binary.

Whether we are heterosexual, homosexual, bisexual, transgender, etc., most of us identify as male or female. But not everyone feels that they fit neatly into a category of "man" or "woman" or "male" or "female." Some people are of a gender that is neither male nor female or one that blends parts of being a woman and a man. And some don't identify with a gender at all, while others find their gender changes through time.

Those who don't feel that their gender is male or female describe themselves in many different ways, including agender, genderqueer, or bigender. But, by far, the term they use the most is non-binary. While none of those terms share the exact same meaning, they all lend themselves to the experience of being neither male nor female.

Why Non-binary?

Our society is narrow-minded when it comes to genders, only identifying with just two – male and female. This idea that only two genders exist is often called gender binary. The word "binary" means "having two parts," i.e., male and female, so non-binary is used to describe a person who doesn't fall into either one of those categories.

Basic Non-binary Facts

☐ *Non-binary is nothing new* – non-binary identities have been recognized by societies and cultures worldwide for millennia. It isn't anything new, and people are not "confused" or trying to follow the latest fad or trend.

☐ *Some non-binary people undergo surgery to change their bodies to look like the gender they identify with.* Not all non-binary people feel the need for this but, for some, it is a critical procedure for their happiness and fulfillment.

☐ *It's wrong to say that all transgender people are non-binary.* Some are, but most transgender people identify with being male or female and should be treated the same as every other male or female.

☐ *Intersex and non-binary are not the same thing.* Intersex people have genes or anatomy outside of the typical male or female definitions, and most will identify as a man or a woman. However, non-binary people rarely identify as intersex because the bodies they are born with fit the definitions of a man or woman, but their gender identity does not necessarily match their bodies.

Respecting and Supporting Non-binary People

You might think it hard to respect and support those who identify as non-binary, but it's critical that you do just that when your own children identify as such.

- *Understanding is not synonymous with respecting.* While you may not understand why your child has chosen to identify as non-binary, you can still respect them and their choices. Not everyone is aware of non-binary genders, and some don't understand them. That doesn't mean you cannot respect them.

- *Use the name your child asks you to use.* This is possibly the most important aspect of having respect for your non-binary child. The name you gave your child at birth may not reflect the gender they now identify with. If they ask you to use the new name they have chosen for themselves, do so without question.

- *Don't assume a person's gender.* Sure, your child may look like a boy or a girl, but that doesn't mean they identify with that. You should never assume their gender because you cannot tell if they are non-binary just by looking at their appearance.

- *Ask what pronouns you should use.* Not all non-binary people use the same pronouns. Some will continue to use "he/him" or "she/her" while others prefer to use 'they/them." And there are other pronouns they may use too. While you may feel awkward asking your child which pronouns they want you to use, it is a simple thing to do and it shows that you respect their choices.

☐ *Advocate for policies supporting non-binary people.* Your child will want to know that their life, dress, and gender choices are respected and supported at home, at school, and in public.

☐ *Understand that it may be challenging for your child to choose which bathroom they should use.* They may feel unsafe in public bathrooms because of harassment or physical or verbal attacks. Non-binary children should be able to feel safe in whichever bathroom they choose to use.

☐ *Talk to your child.* There isn't a one-size-fits-all philosophy for being non-binary, and the best way to understand is to talk to your child and talk to other non-binary people, listen to them and understand their stories.

Speaking of stories, each chapter of this guide is a personal story from a parent of a non-binary child or from the child's point of view. All of your questions are answered by them, including how to support your child, how to approach telling others, understand pronouns, and much more.

CHAPTER 1

Simone's Story – Making It Public

Tough chapter to start with but let's just get to it first – your child is non-binary, and you need to let everyone know.

Simone had to take her daughter to the dentist. They needed to get a new retainer and make sure that it fit properly. You see, their faithful family dog had decided it would be good fun to chew up her daughter's old one. Her daughter was devastated when they found the chewed up retainer. They'd been very responsible, kept it safe, and out of harm's way, or so they thought. They never lost it and always took good care of it.

About a year ago, the dentist told them that Charlie, Simone's daughter, would need an appointment to be fitted for braces. So, as she paid for the retainer, she mentioned to the receptionist that she needed to set up an appointment.

No problem, the receptionist said and asked what the child's name was. Simone replied, "Charlie, with the same last name."

When Charlie was born, they were named Charles. That's right. Her daughter was born a boy but was delighted that many people had started mistaking them for a girl. When they asked Charles what they should do when people called them a girl, they said they should just go with it. They didn't mind being mistaken for a girl, but they had made it clear that they will never transition to female – they doesn't want to actually be a girl.

—————————— ⌘ ——————————

This is where things get quite complicated. The notion of gender is rather deeply ingrained into us in one way while, in another way, it isn't. Where Simone lives, they often run into people they've known for a long time. Right up to fifth grade, Charlie was using he/him pronouns, and they were never mistaken for being a girl. Then they suddenly changed. They started to present as a female, growing their hair long, wearing girl's clothes from a girl's clothing store. They wore headbands with big purple flowers on them, sparkly pink Sketchers, girls t-shirts, jeggings, and girls sweatpants – to anyone who didn't know them, they looked like a girl. But they weren't. Charlie was and is a boy, and for a while, they continued to use he/him/his pronouns. Then he started using they/them pronouns, and everything changed.

Kids find it hard to be private about gender. They can't do what an adult can do – pick up and move somewhere different, start a new life as the gender they want to be, somewhere anonymous, where no one knows them. And other kids often have no clue of the distinction between the sex assigned at birth and the gender the child feels they are. To be fair, most adults are unaware of that distinction too. If it isn't obvious at first glance, a child will come right out and ask another child if they are a boy or girl. Adults are a little more diplomatic.

With young kids, it's even harder, partly because elementary schools still use gender-segregated practices – how often have you heard them say, "boys in one line, girls in another?" Or, "sit in a circle, boy/girl/boy/girl?" Any gender-segregated practice is a reminder to a non-binary child that schools often don't see their gender identity as important – they are what they were assigned at birth, and that's it.

Back to Simone.

The receptionist asked Simone when his birthday was. Charlie, Simone's daughter, does not particularly like having unwanted attention drawn to her, and they could see what was about to happen. They asked Simone if they could go wait in the car and, while they was rarely allowed to stay in the car alone, Simone made an exception this time.

Simone leaned towards the receptionist and whispered that Charlie was not a he. Charlie was non-binary and used they/them pronouns. The receptionist tilted her head and looked at her questioningly. Simone continued, saying that she knows it wasn't the easiest of conversations to have but that she would appreciate the receptionist helping out as best she could in terms of the records they kept.

The receptionist nodded, apparently reassuring Simone that she understood, and then focused back on her computer. She was more than likely considering her options, and then, with some hesitation, she asked if she should refer to Charlie as "she.". Simone looked at her and said, "No." She explained to the receptionist that Charlie was non-binary, neither female nor male, and was gender nonconforming. Still the receptionist didn't understand, so Simone continued explaining because it seemed like the appointment couldn't be made until they'd settled on the pronouns.

Although Charlie had been assigned male when they were born, Simone explained that they now presented and expressed themselves like a girl. But, she also explained, Charlie wasn't prepared to transition to female, so they found themselves in a tough situation where Charlie doesn't feel like a boy or a girl, but a person. While Simone was talking, she noticed that the other receptionist was making a point of listening to the conversation.

It was clear to Simone that this was new to them so, she decided to tone things down to a level where she felt they would understand her easier. She explained that Charlie was 11 and might be transgender or might not be. The two ladies understood this, and the second one began nodding to indicate her understanding. Then the first receptionist said "oh," and frowned as if to say, "oh, you poor woman." Simone smiled at her and explained she was just trying to be a supportive parent.

The first receptionist smiled and said quietly that they had patients who were transitioning but always used boy or girl pronouns. She said that was why she was confused because they had never had any patients who used non-binary pronouns. Simone kind of smiled and told them that now they did.

All that said, they still hadn't settled on the pronouns. Without words being spoken, Simone understood that the receptionist was telling her there was no "they/them" option, not even an option for "other" in their drop-down gender list. Simone needed to fill the silence, so, not wanting to ask them to do more work and wanting to keep the peace, she explained that Charlie might transition, she may not. Or she may stay non-binary for the rest of her life. As Charlie was only 11, she explained that they weren't ready to make any major decisions right now.

Simone noticed that she had the full attention of both receptionists now. They were both nodding, appearing to validate something Simone was NOT trying to say. Simone realized that she had come across as implying that her daughter was too young for a sex change, which is not what she was trying to say. Unwittingly, she had perpetuated the false narrative of kids not knowing their gender because they were too young.

One said to Simone that she got it, that she knew it was hard to make these big decisions, while the other said that they couldn't imagine how confused that child must be. Simone tried to go back, saying it wasn't confusion, but the receptionist cut her off, saying confusion was the wrong word. She said she imagined that Simone must go everywhere, not knowing what reactions she would get or whether other people would understand.

Laughing, the receptionist said, "and all you wanted to do was make an appointment!" Simone also laughed and said it was hard to know who will be accepting, and the receptionist looked at her and said that it should never be that way.

After taking a minute to think, she decided to place a personal note on Charlie's file that only the dentist would see. She checked with Simone that what she had written was right – it was. After passing along the insurance details and her phone number, Simone made the appointment and left.

As she walked out the door, she berated herself for not choosing from a small list of trans-friendly dentists, even if she would have had to travel an hour for the appointment. She felt that she had made a hash up of explaining it and hoped she would do better next time.

Simone realized she had left her daughter in the car for more than half an hour but didn't want to tell her she had spent most of that time negotiating pronouns. Charlie didn't want anyone to make a fuss, especially since most older teens got pronouns without needing to explain. Simone couldn't tell Charlie that she had unintentionally made a mess of the quick in-and-out appointment by having to explain pronouns, so she just said that they were booked up and it was difficult to find something that worked for all parties.

Because, when it comes down to it, that was the truth.

As I said, this may have been a strange story to start this book with, but it clearly demonstrates one of the hardest issues that you will have – trying to explain to people that your child is non-binary and discussing pronouns. Some people will get it and accept it, while others won't.

Throughout this book, we'll see more stories from people who will tell you what it was like to explain this to others. First, though, we're heading over to talk to Max about pronouns.

CHAPTER 2

Max's Story – Which Pronouns Do I Use?

"Dad, I need to tell you something. I'm gender-fluid."

Max had been engrossed in reading a magazine when his daughter made her announcement. He looked up at her – not in shock or horror, but in anticipation of the conversation he'd known was coming for months. And now it was here. The first thing he said to his daughter was, "tell me what that means."

15-year-old Jennifer repeated that she was gender-fluid, sometimes feeling like a girl, sometimes like a boy. Feeling his stomach tighten up, Max said to her, "a boy? Really?"

"Yes," said Jennifer. She smiled at him and told him she wanted to change her name to Jordan, but before she could finish the sentence, he told her he thought that was too big a decision for a sophomore in high school to make.

But Jennifer/Jordan was absolutely certain. As certain as she was when she told her father that, from now on, she was using the personal pronouns, they/them.

This is a common conversation now, between parents and their children the world over. Children or teens are trying to tell their parents that they want to change their names and use pronouns that better reflect the gender they identify with. And even if your child never tells you this themselves, there is a very good chance that they know someone who has changed their name and taken on new pronouns.

If you are reading this book, your child has already approached you, or you have a pretty good idea that they will, and you want to know how to deal with the situation. Many people find it hard to keep up with changes in gender identity, and some even find it hard to accept. It doesn't matter how confused the topic makes you. The fact is that gender fluidity, and new pronouns are here to stay, and the first step to understanding it is to grasp how scientists understand gender.

A paper titled "The Biological Contributions to Gender Identity and Gender Diversity" was published in the Behavior Genetics journal by the American Psychological Society. In it, gender identity is defined as "a person's deeply-felt, inherent sense of being a boy, a man, or a male; a girl, a woman, or a female; or an alternative gender (e.g., genderqueer, gender non-conforming, gender-neutral) that may or may not correspond to a person's sex assigned at birth or to a person's primary or secondary sex characteristics."

The University of Connecticut Rainbow Center has produced a Gender & Pronoun Guide where they explain that there are three independent gender aspects:

1. *Biological sex,* relating to genital anatomy

2. *Gender expression,* relating to how a person represents themselves to others

3. *Gender identity,* relation to how a person senses their own gender.

When a person identifies as bi-gender or androgyne, it indicates they have a combination of male and female characteristics. When a person identifies as agender, they don't identify with either mainstream gender, and gender-fluidity is when they move between male and female characteristics. Lastly, genderqueer or non-binary indicates a person who doesn't identify as female or male.

When a person identifies as non-binary, they ask people to use gender-neutral pronouns when referring to them. The most common non-binary pronouns are they/them, but there are plenty of others, as you will see later.

This new etiquette may seem challenging to you, especially when it's your own kids. You might even secretly hope that these new gender pronouns are just a passing phase and will eventually fade away. Stop right there. It's time to accept that things are changing, and this is not one of those phases.

Pew Research recently did a survey, revealing that around 35% of those born after 1996 (Generation Z) said they knew of someone who used gender-neutral pronouns, and 59% said that forms should be adapted to provide gender options other than Male or Female.

Many institutions have gone down the route of adapting their policies to fit the new gender landscape. Ten years ago, the University of Vermont changed its policies to indicate a neutral gender when students register. In 2015, Harvard followed suit, and now, more than 20 campuses and over 50 schools provide students with different gender options. In 2014 Facebook added over 50 different gender options, while Lyft now provides gender-neutral pronouns on their app. United Airlines provides non-binary booking options, and many states allow people to change the gender listed on their birth certificates.

Gender-neutral pronouns are here to stay – it's time to get used to it and accept it.

Should your child ask you to use these new pronouns with them or with one of their friends, you will undoubtedly find it odd at first. After all, you've always used he/him/his or she/her/hers pronouns– that's what you were taught. You might find it somewhat unnerving, and you probably won't understand how your child could possibly feel this way.

Think about it this way – when your child asks you to use different pronouns, there is way more at stake than awkward feelings and poor grammar. By using your child's chosen pronouns, you are affirming and validating two things – their gender identity and your support of it. When your kid hears you using the right pronouns, it is clear to them that you support their choices, which makes things easier for them.

If your child identifies as non-binary and you don't use the right pronouns, you will make them feel unwelcome. It could even make them feel as though they are invisible, that you don't really see them for who they really are. If you misgender your child, it could even hurt them and your relationship with them, irreparably in some cases.

Here are some real-life stories from children and young adults who identify as non-binary and how they feel about personal pronouns.

Jackie is a film student at San Francisco State, a non-binary using they/them as their pronouns. Via a text message, Jackie said it is painful to be misgendered, not to mention uncomfortable. When you don't feel as though people see you, it wears you down, and going for long periods being misgendered can lead to depression because you feel invisible or that people don't accept you for who you are and think you should be a "normal" male or female. When family and friends use the right pronouns, Jackie says they feel as though they see her and love them for who they are.

Kieran is 15 and lives in Missouri. Ten years ago, Kieran was called Keira, and he feels uncomfortable when people misgender him. He says he doesn't want excuses, such as "we're older, we're not used to this" or "it's just too hard to remember." He thinks people should make an effort – it's no different than knowing that person's name, after all, and when the right pronouns are used, he feels great, knowing that people are making an effort to really see him.

Jay is a 19-year-old Oberlin College student, and they say their family and close friends still misgender them accidentally, using he/him and not they/them. They know that people make mistakes and a quick apology and use of the correct pronouns go a long way towards making them feel better. But when people continually use the wrong pronouns, it makes them feel as though their identity has been called into question. In their mind, if their personal pronouns cannot be respected, it means their identity isn't respected, and neither are they.

So, is it really so hard for you to switch from he/him/his or she/

her/hers to they/them? It is, and Kieran's dad will freely admit that, even though he try hard, he still trips up occasionally. His wife is far better at it than he is. If people try but get it wrong a few times, it's fine, so long as they keep trying and eventually get there.

So, when your child starts that conversation about gender, what should you do? Here are some tips to help you along:

- Whatever you do, don't freak out!

- Sit down with them and listen to what your child says and why they feel this way. By all means, ask questions, but only for clarification purposes. Never judge.

- Tell your child you are grateful that they trusted you enough to tell you.

- Tell them you will do your best, but it won't be easy, so it's okay for them to correct you. Tell them you will always do your best and ask them how you can do this.

- A few weeks after the conversation, sit down and talk to them again, ask them how they think you are doing. Ask if there is anything that you can be doing better.

- Talk to other family members and friends, and help them adjust too.

Although it seems like being non-binary came from nowhere, it's important to realize that it isn't just a phase or a fad. Non-binary people have existed worldwide for thousands of years, and, in time, they/them will be as accepted as pronouns just like he/him and she/her.

Why Pronouns Are Important

When you use the right pronouns for whomever you are talking to, you show them that you respect them and that you are fully including them in your life. The one thing you must never do is assume pronouns. When you assume your child's pronouns, you send them a message that a person must look a certain way to use those pronouns.

It can cause serious offense, even harm, to use the wrong pronouns. When you ignore what your child is asking you to do, you imply that they do not exist, that you are pushing their request to one side, and ignoring everything they gathered up the courage to tell you.

A study in 2016 found that when a person's pronouns are affirmed, their gender identity is affirmed too. This can lead to fewer cases of depression and higher self-esteem. It makes the person feel comfortable with their appearance and how they identify their gender.

Sex and Gender

Many people use these two words interchangeably, but that is wrong – they both have different meanings. Gender is classed as a social construct and used to denote the cultural and social role of sex within the community.

Gender identity and expression are often developed in response to an environment, referring to how a person identifies themselves on the gender spectrum – and yes, there is such a thing. We'll briefly describe it now but go into more detail later on.

Gender is not divided neatly into two categories – male and female. Some don't identify with either of those, while others identify with both. The only person who can determine their gender identity is the person themselves and, while they may identify with a specific gender, this may change to another gender or to no specific gender over time.

Being Inclusive and Respectful

So, how do you do this with your child?

Well, the first thing to do is to take note of their pronouns and not assume them. For any other person you are talking to, if you can't be sure of their pronouns, use they/them. When you use gender-neutral pronouns, you are not assuming that person's gender. You are not making any assumptions about jobs like you do when you use "he" when you talk about a doctor or "she" when talking about a receptionist.

To be honest, the easiest thing to do is ask your child what their pronouns are and how they want you to use them. That way, your child knows that you respect them and that you support their choices.

The Commonly Used Pronouns

The most common pronouns that we all know are he, she, and they, and some examples of how they are used include:

- [ ] He laughed at the movie with his friends, thoroughly enjoying himself.

- [ ] She laughed at the movie with her friends, thoroughly enjoying herself.

- [ ] They laughed at the movie with their friends, thoroughly enjoying themselves.

However, people use many more pronouns, and your child may choose one of these. The table below is not an exhaustive list, but it does show the most common pronouns used today:

He/She/ They	Him/Her/ Them	His/Hers/ Theirs	Himself/ Herself/ Themself
co	co	cos	coself
en	en	ens	enself
ey	em	eirs	emself
xie	hire (here)	hirs	hirself
yo	yo	yos	yoself
ze	zir	zirs	zirself
ve	vis	ver	verself

So, we can now put these into the example sentence from above:

- **Ze** laughed at the movie with zir friends, thoroughly enjoying **zirself.**

- **Xie** laughed at the movie with hire friends, thoroughly enjoying **hirself.**

- **Co** laughed at the movie with co friends, thoroughly enjoying **coself.**

What to Do If You Use the Wrong Pronouns by Mistake

No matter how hard you try, this is a new situation for you, and you are bound to make mistakes in the pronouns you use. When you do, recognize that you have, quickly apologize, use the right pronouns, and continue with your conversation.

I say quickly apologize because too much can be a bad thing. If you use the wrong pronoun with your child and make a long bumbling apology, you put them in the embarrassing position of having to tell you to stop. It also places them squarely in a spotlight they may not have wanted to be in.

Your child should feel comfortable enough to correct your mistakes and help you remember the right pronouns. What they won't be happy with is continuous misuse.

General Do's And Do Not's

When your child has broken the news about their new identity, there are some things you need to do and things you definitely must NOT do:

- ☐ Make sure you know their pronouns

- ☐ Take the time to practice those pronouns in private to lessen the chances of mistakes

- ☐ ~~Apologize~~ *Correct yourself & move on* if you use the wrong pronoun. *If you are corrected, say thank you & move on. (cont below)*

- ☐ Do not assume pronouns based on what you see

- ☐ Do not ignore it when you use the wrong pronoun by mistake

- ☐ Do not assume that their pronouns will stay the same

- ☐ Do not use the terms "masculine" and "feminine" to describe pronouns

Follow these, and you are less likely to make mistakes when it comes to your child's pronouns.

Let's move on to Sandy's story. It's full of advice on how to tell others about your child's decision.

Apologizing puts the ~~person~~ person in the position of telling you, "It's OK," when it's not. Thank you means you understand your mistake & appreciate the correction.

CHAPTER 3

Sandy's Story – Telling Others

Sandy's daughter, Toni, is seven, and they use gender-neutral pronouns. Toni was six when they first started to use the pronoun "they" when talking about themselves and asked their parents to use the same pronoun. Both agreed, but, at the time, they didn't give it much thought.

However, a few months down the line, Toni, otherwise referred to as T, returned from school in a pretty distressed state, saying that their classmates and teachers were not using the right pronouns. At that point, Sandy and her husband realized they needed to sit down and talk to T.

They sat and talked, asking T about gender identity, how T saw themself, and what T felt, and learned that T no longer identified with the gender we always knew them as, the gender they were assigned at birth. T said they felt like nothing more than a person, a human being.

That was all T's mom needed to hear. Over time, she and her husband talked more with T and watched as their child settled into a non-binary identity quite comfortably. She says that all they did was send a clear message to T that they loved them, they're always there for them, and they're always willing to listen to anything they had to say. They also said they would check in on T regularly to ensure their mental health was thriving and that they were not struggling.

The American Psychological Association fully supports this approach and has found that the health and well-being of children are much better when families provide full support and affirmation for their child's gender identity.

Sadly, their family and closest friends didn't share that support, and both Sandy and her husband have found themselves having to protect T from the intolerance shown by some family members.

Our children should be treated with kindness and respect, no matter what gender they identify with.

Sandy says that she and her husband have taken the worst of their family's pushback, most of which has come from their respective mothers. Both women spend inordinate amounts of time and energy telling them that they don't believe T knows what they are doing, that T is far too young to decide something like that, and, in some cases, that T is talking utter nonsense. Do they know how damaging it is to T to have both their grandmothers' acting like this?

Both parents have expended a great deal of emotional labor on asserting their child's autonomy but say that they will assert much more if it means T can live peacefully as the person they identify with. They shouldn't have to struggle to ensure T is treated with kindness and respect, especially not from their own families, regardless of the gender they identify with.

T fully understands their own gender identity and knows that they are loved, respected, heard, seen, and fully accepted within their own home. But Sandy says that was the easy bit. The hard part comes when you have to persuade the rest of the family to treat T the same way.

Let's Get Talking

When it comes to talking to other adults in your family about your child's identity, it can be a very difficult conversation, one of the hardest you are likely to have. Grandparents, in particular, tend to be far more conservative in their ideas of gender and will not find it easy to understand your child's decision, let alone accept it.

Advocating for your child is also very difficult when you are defending them from your own family. The best way to approach this is to be patient and compassionate, not defensive and confrontational.

Situations You Should Prepare For

☐ *Problems with terminology* – not everyone understands the terminology and pronouns that come with non-binary gender identity, and some will find it hard to understand and grasp these pronouns. They may use terns that were once accepted but are now seen as derogatory or offensive, and it will certainly take them some time to understand why preferred personal pronouns are so important. So long as they show they are making an effort to accept and

19

change, show patience with them while firmly correcting their use of pronouns and terminology.

☐ *Family get-togethers, holidays, and gifts* – if your child's non-binary expression is new, you need to have that talk with the family before a get-together. Otherwise, the conversations may be upsetting and contentious, especially if held in front of your child. If you are aware of a family get-together coming up, talk to the rest of the family one-to-one beforehand. Explain that your child has identified as non-binary and what it means. Ask that they respect your child's request for personal pronouns. Try to find allies, those that understand and accept what is happening. Ask them to help you with these difficult conversations. When it comes to buying gifts, request that clothing fits with your child's gender identity – if they don't want to do that, ask for gifts that aren't gender-specific, such as art supplies, books, and so on.

☐ *Family who refuses to accept your child's identity* – one or more family members are likely to tell you that it's all a load of rubbish, and they won't accept the new pronouns or gender identity. This could mean they go as far as deliberately misgendering, trying to get your child to change and conform to their assigned gender, right down to small, unnoticeable acts of aggression that a young child may not understand or even notice. Situations like this require that you, as the parent, step in and determine what your child needs, even if it means having to sever all ties with that family member, as hard as that may be. Sometimes, those who find it hard to accept at the start will change their minds as time goes on. In this case, you should continue to support, love, and accept your non-binary child openly in the hope that other people come around to your way of thinking.

Talking Points

When you have that conversation with your family and friends, remember that this is the same child you have raised since birth, the same child you have always known and always loved – the only difference is in gender identity. Often, it helps if you can explain things like the difference between gender and sex or what gender dysphoria is – the unease a person may feel when they don't feel their biological assigned sex and their gender identity match. By educating yourself before you talk to people, you can show your support and show that you have made sure you fully understand it.

Also, remember that your child is happy. Many parents whose children come out as non-binary have found that their child is much happier and more relaxed when they can live openly as the gender they identify with. If this applies to you, point out to your family that you are providing your child with your unequivocal support and that they are much happier because of it.

Some people will try to tell you that you are a bad parent or that your child isn't right. Ignore them. There is nothing wrong with how you have brought up your child, and there is nothing wrong with your child. That kind of thing can seriously harm a person during the time they need most validation and support the most. There is no point in trying to make your child into the gender they were assigned at birth if that isn't what they feel they are. Not only is it cruel, but it can also permanently damage their mental health, and that is the last thing you want for your child.

So, be fully supportive of your child and be firm when you are telling your family. If they cannot or will not accept that your child is non-binary, then you may have to take the tough step of cutting them off until they can accept it. That's for your child's sake, not yours.

Next, we have Tilly's story. She's a non-binary adult. In this chapter, you'll find plenty of tips on parenting non-binary kids.

CHAPTER 4

Tilly's Story – Non-binary Kids Need Support and Space

Tilly came out as non-binary when she was a child. However, while she had wonderful loving parents, they didn't have the sort of information and support available to parents of non-binary kids today. Tilly says she suffered because of it, and she doesn't want any other kids to go through what she did.

Tilly says her parents didn't really understand her, and they certainly didn't understand what non-binary meant. She was forced to act like the girl she was born as, the sex she was assigned at birth. It was rough for her, and she really struggled it understand how other girls could act like girls with so little effort when she found it so hard – she simply didn't identify with being female.

Yes, she felt uncomfortable at constantly being called "young lady," and yes, she struggled to deal with hair that wouldn't do what she wanted it to do, but the worst of it, in her own words, was "I felt like I was playing a role I hadn't chosen, let alone rehearsed for."

Think about that when your child tells you they are non-binary.

Tilly says that, as a non-binary child raised as a female, she felt a lot of emotions. She felt confused and sad when told to like feminine things, and she felt that she was constantly disappointing her family. The style she developed due to this could only be called "anti-girl," and even she says it wasn't a good look.

It wasn't until she went to college that she began choosing her own clothes, clothes that she felt good wearing and that looked good on her. It took her so long because she felt she had been brainwashed into believing that, if she tried hard enough, one day she would be comfortable wearing typical "girl clothes."

And that experience has taught her that children should be given a gender-neutral environment in which to find themselves and the gender they feel they should be. Not a gender-neutral environment, that is not the same as a gender-free environment.

Tilly also says that non-binary kids should be given the support they need to determine their own gender identity. When you give them space to explore, they can find their gender and determine how they want to express it, and they start to make the choices they feel good about, not the ones they are expected to make.

One of the most important parts of anyone's childhood is discovering how uplifting and joyful self-expression is. Gender-neutral parenting lets your kids be themselves – if they want to carry a handbag to their karate lessons, let them – it lets your child be who they want to be without fearing the reaction and shame from their family and friends.

Tilly's childhood taught her that parents of non-binary kids need to make life easier for their kids – easier than hers was – and these are six ways you can do that:

1. Allow Your Child the Space They Need to Be Themselves

When your child is born, the first thing your family and friends do is give gifts based on gender. Parents do the same thing – they paint the nursery blue for a boy and pink for a girl, and they buy gendered clothing. Gendered roles are the norm, and, gradually, a picture develops of what the baby will be like, based on its assigned gender. For example, "my son will be an engineer when he grows up" or "my daughter will go to ballet classes and look beautiful in pink tutus." It could be that your daughter becomes the engineer and your son wears the pink tutus, but the behavior of treating your child as the gender they were assigned at birth can continue for a long time. Kids who don't feel like they fit as a "boy" or a "girl" will end up confused, isolated, and sad which inevitably leads to serious mental health issues.

Tilly didn't align with the gender she was assigned at birth. It wasn't just the girl things that upset her. It was more the alienation she felt and the feeling that she wasn't good at being what she was born as, and that it was her fault.

The thing is, all kids are different, and all kids like different things. Rather than buying gendered clothing, toys, etc., keep things neutral. Allow your child to be in the driving seat, allow them to discover what books they want to read, what clothes to wear, games to play, and so on. Just let them discover what they like doing and being.

If your child identifies with the gender they were assigned with, sure, go ahead and buy gendered clothing and toys but only if it comes from them, not because you think it's what they should have.

The easiest place to start is with gender-neutral toys. Should your child want a toy that doesn't fit with the perceived notion of their assigned gender, such as your son wanting a Barbie doll, then go with it and honor it as you would honor your son's request for an action man toy.

Above all, do not give your non-binary child special treatment – the last thing they want is attention being drawn to them. Just treat them as you would any other child but honor their wishes, even if their requests don't fit with what you think your child should want.

2. Teach Your Kids to Question Societal Expectations of Gender

Assigned genders are coming into question more and more these days, and it's important that you let your child know your house is a place where they can express their wishes and thoughts freely, without fear of judgment, and a place where they can think about the choices they make.

Children who can think critically are better equipped to work out what they want. While this is useful advice for any parent, it is more helpful for parents of non-binary kids. At some point, your non-binary child is going to spend a significant amount of time working out who they really are and fighting societal norms.

As their parent, you can make life easier for them if you teach them to question these norms and think about what works for them. It could be as simple as them learning to question stereotypes, such as "Simon says girls can't play cricket." If your child says this, or something like it, ask them why they think Simon said that. Teach them that they do not have to take everything in life at face value.

3. Be Honest With Them About How Others Will React to Their Choices

That includes family, friends, classmates, even their teachers.

People are stuck on gender stereotyping. In many ways, you will find it easier to accept your non-binary child if their new values and tastes are close to or are the same as the gender norms than if their tastes are the opposite of what you expect.

Obviously, it all comes down to community and what your child identifies with, but most people are more comfortable when a person fits the pre-determined categories.

Some people find non-binary children quite uncomfortable to accept and be around but, even if you mean well, even if you try to act like you accept your child, you can still make them feel excluded. It's hard to get away from ingrained ideas about boys and girls, and you could end up forcing your child to accept your ideas instead of their own, which can be immensely damaging.

It is not unheard of for people to get frustrated or angry when confronted with a child who doesn't fit their ideas of gender norms. As a parent, that is a dangerous attitude to have. Not only do you risk your child's mental health, but you also risk pushing them away for good, especially when they are at the age where they want to please you – your rejection of their values is excruciatingly painful to them.

While we have no way of controlling how people behave when they meet your child, you can control how you behave. You can also make it clear to your child that you have their back, that they have your unequivocal support, and allow them to choose how they interact with others.

Sure, it will be tough at first. You want to protect them from a cold, cruel world, but you also want them to be true to themselves.

Perhaps one of the most important things you can do is tell your child that, while they have your support, not everyone is open-minded enough to accept that they are non-binary.

Help your child decide which battles to fight and which ones to walk away from. Reinforce that they have your support at all times.

4. Let Your Child Have a Say in What They Will Wear

When you go to buy clothes for your child, take them with you. Let them choose their clothes themselves but strike a compromise on clothes for formal events.

Again, all parents should allow their children to choose what to wear, within reason, but for non-binary children, this is a huge issue.

Tilly remembers too well how her little brother got upset when he was punished for shaving his armpits. He didn't end up identifying as non-binary, but it was his choice to shave. However, because it went against the preconceived notions, he was shamed by a family member.

That kind of thing is always happening to non-binary children.

As their parent, it is up to you to provide a safe space and be the person who supports their child's exploration. The rest of the world will be negative enough – you don't want to be your child's first bully.

You should prepare for the fact that your child may change their mind or, at different times, they may want different things.

Tilly was very feminine as a preschooler. She loved those cute little dresses, the more sparkles and ruffles, the better. As she got older, her style changed, and she knew that skirts weren't for her by the time she reached middle school. However, she still felt she was under overwhelming pressure to wear them, and she did – the results weren't pretty.

Most kids experience a change in taste and style, and some will have a different one from one day to the next. The most important thing to do is remain steadfast in your support and love, regardless of why your child makes the choices they do. Help them make empowered and informed decisions about their appearance.

5. Make Sure Your Non-binary Child Is Exposed to Media About Non-binary People

Everybody needs to see themselves as some kind of hero, an adult, and a member of their community.

When Tilly was young, she liked girls, but she was taught that lesbians were unnatural. She knew two – both were in their fifties, and neither was attractive to look at. They were the only two lesbians she knew. She had never seen them in television programs, never read about them in books, and, once she was old enough to buy books for herself, she found she was ashamed of buying those containing any LGBTIQ+ characters. She would pay for them and hide them so her mother couldn't see them.

Media representation is a big part of our lives, and it is important to kids, especially non-binary kids who don't know any other non-binary people. Most of us are surrounded by role models our whole lives, and it's hard to have to start thinking about how important they are. If you were a girl, assigned at birth and remaining that way, with a tough mother, a lovely bubbly aunt, or a hard teacher, you might have had them as role models. As a non-binary, your child doesn't have that in their everyday life, so it's down to you to make sure you find that for them elsewhere.

6. You Are Your Child's Advocate

It's your job to educate your family, friends, your child's school friends and their parents, and the school teachers. Children aren't always able to advocate for themselves – they may not be old enough to express their needs and wants, or they may not understand the principles adults live by. If they request something that doesn't fit with people's expectations, they won't be taken seriously.

You are their ally, possibly the only one they have. You can explain to others why your child needs to use the "wrong" bathroom, you can insist on the enforcement of laws designed to protect your child, and you can interfere when other people are hostile or ignorant towards your child's choices.

You have that power; use it for the good of your child.

Support Is the Most Important Thing You Can Do

Non-binary children will face challenges their whole life, depending on the sex they were assigned at birth.

For example, a feminine child who was assigned as a male at birth will almost certainly be teased, even bullied for their femininity. In some cases, they may even be brutalized, physically and emotionally, by people who want to get them to toughen up, to be the boy they were born.

A child assigned female but who has masculine traits will often be tolerated as being a bit of a tomboy, but only if they are the right age, race, and the right kind of a tomboy. However, when they step away from behavior expected of them as a female by being bisexual, non-straight, non-binary, or by continuing to act like a boy when they reach their teenage years, that tolerance disappears.

Overall, non-binary children with neither a definite male nor female identity are often considered to be confused, not old enough to know what they want.

Don't be that parent.

The only solution to ending the discrimination against non-binary people is to stop seeing a newborn child's genitals as the defining factor of the sex they will be their entire lives. As it is likely to be a long time before that happens, the next best thing is to support your child, especially when they have the guts to go against a system that defines them by preconceived norms and tries to deny them the opportunity to be themselves.

Next, we meet Julie, who has some advice on supporting non-binary kids in a gender binary world.

CHAPTER 5

Julie's Story – Supporting Your Non-binary Child in a Gender Binary World

*Julie prefers to keep herself and her child anonymous, so names have been changed to protect them.

Julie is somewhat unclear on how their journey began. She remembers Sprout being in the third grade when they started saying they felt like a girl inside. That was the year they made some new friends, older friends who could act as mentors because they were genderqueer and transgender. Suddenly, Julie found she had tons of questions she needed answers to, mainly on how to support Sprout. She also knew that she had no clue where to even begin.

She says she can only talk about her own experiences, not those of other parents in similar situations. All parents who embark on this journey will have their experiences, and no two will be the same. To that end, she says that the knowledge she is imparting should only be used as a guide – if something isn't working, don't do it. Find your own way, knowing that you have the support you need.

Why Anonymity?

You might think Julie is ashamed of her child, but she isn't. In fact, she says she's never been prouder. The anonymity is at the request of Sprout because they choose to make their gender identity a private matter for their own reasons. You'll figure most of those out throughout this chapter.

She also makes it clear that this story is not about her, nor is she trying to "out" her child publicly. All she wants to do is share her experiences and ensure other parents have someone they can relate to.

Why Non-binary? Why Not Transgender?

Because Sprout isn't transgender, that's why. Sprout has declared a non-binary identity and, as Julie has no idea what raising a transgender child is like, she can't talk about it. She also learned that resources for children who come out as non-binary are incredibly limited in so many ways. So often, comments we hear are aimed at forcing children into the gender binary, regardless of how they feel.

It's important to understand that there is a difference between transgender and non-binary, and so many people muddle them up. Society finds it easier to understand transgender because a transgender person is a male or female. Non-binary is different, falling in an area people typically do not understand. Most of society accepts the genders of male or female because they understand this. They have been brought up with there being two genders. Non-binary falls in the middle, and most people will shy away from this. They tend to see how your child presents – Sprout presents as a male, feels like a female inside and identifies as non-binary. Julie has lost count of the number of times people have told her that Sprout "needs to start acting like the boy he is" or "it's only a phase, he'll get over it."

That is not how Sprout feels.

Here's another way that Julie says transgender and non-binary differ.

Sprout can easily pass as a male, and they are fine with that. In fact, Sprout doesn't want people to think any different because they don't want more problems. They won't be taking part in Pride, and they won't be a part of any community. It's quite simple – non-binary is neither male nor female. It's not gay, lesbian, bi, or trans. It's in a grey category all of its own.

Parents with non-binary children are on a different journey. They are not fighting the same fight as everyone else. Even in the LGBTIQ+ community, non-binary people don't feel like they have a voice, and, as parents, that makes it very difficult to support your child.

It Isn't About You

That's the first thing Julie tells parents of non-binary children. Society places a great deal of pressure on parents to believe that their parenting is reflected in their children. The parents make decisions, occasionally based on the way others see them through their child's behavior. If a child is fighting with other children in the playground, it must be the parent's fault. If the child kicks off and starts screaming in the restaurant? It's the parent's fault. And if a child isn't doing so well at school, that must be the parents' fault too.

Julie stresses that absolutely nothing about the gender identity your child has is about you - it's all about them.

Most parents would do anything to protect their kids from bullies, stalkers, and murderers because their lives and safety must come first. When your child expresses themselves as non-binary, well, you need to do the same thing.

These days, it can be a matter of life or death for non-binary or transgender kids. The Human Rights Campaign shared some chilling statistics in 2018 in terms of non-binary and transgender youth suicides. They said that more than 50% of male and almost 30% of female transgender teens in the survey admitted that they had attempted suicide. In the non-binary participants, nearly 42% said they had tried to commit suicide at least once.

If you, as a parent, would take a bullet for your child (and I mean that literally), then you need to be the one that stands with them in support against the kind of world that will force them into feeling so bad that suicide is the only option.

Saving their lives requires us to put our feelings aside.

Talk to Others Having the Same Experience

Julie felt lucky to have a network of family and friends she could talk to, people that understood. She has learned from other peoples' experiences and has found it much easier to support

Sprout and ensure they feel comfortable enough at home to be who they are and talk about things bothering them.

She talked to genderqueer and transgender people she made friends with. She talked to their parents. She listened to what they said and learned how they felt when they came out to others. She listened to parents' stories of struggling to change their own perspectives on their children. In short, she learned that she would never let her child struggle if she could help it and to provide Sprout with unequivocal, unwavering support in all their decisions and choices.

Talk About Pronouns

Now that Julie had some education under her belt, she decided it was time to chat with Sprout about pronouns. Sprout was just 7-years-old, and they only knew of the two pronouns – he and she. However, they didn't particularly feel like they were either of them. Sure, they felt like a boy in some things, but, in others, they felt like a girl.

Julie talked with them about why they felt like a boy – two things came up – penis and athleticism. And, why they were a girl – aesthetics or kindness came up.

Some of their non-binary identity qualities could be social structures, such as kindness being feminine and athleticism being masculine (in some places). Sprout was adamant that they felt both ways.

Julie talked about using gender-neutral pronouns, and Sprout opted to use "they."

That night, Julie and her husband started using "they" as Sprout's personal pronouns. They did find it a tough change and sometimes forgot, but they apologize to Sprout and use the right pronoun when they do.

Ask Your Child

All children are different. Sprout was over the moon when their parents started to use "they," but the area they live in is binary gender conforming. As time went by, Sprout found it harder to talk publicly about their gender identity. Their friends didn't understand. Their teachers found it hard to explain it to others and support their choices. They did try, but it's a general failure in society that teachers aren't given the right training and words to explain gender identity to young children.

Sprout made a decision – in private, at home, Sprout would use "they," but, in public, they would use "he."

So Julie and her husband supported his decision. Yes, it was harder. They wanted to provide the right support for Sprout without disrespecting them, but code-switching, i.e., using different pronouns in different places, is why mistakes are made. But, remember, it's about them and what they want, not about us as parents.

Touch Base

Anyone with children knows that it's sometimes hard to get them to talk to you. Sometimes, when Julie asked Sprout what they did at school," the response she would get was "nothing."

Other times though, she might get long conversations about what went on at school when they have their evening cuddles. In the car, they talk deeply about things. When they are playing in the yard, Sprout comes out with all kinds of information they won't give out when Julie asks specific questions.

The trick is to know when your child is in a receptive mood and then talk to them. When Julie asks Sprout if their chosen pronoun is still "they," she isn't showing him disrespect. She just wants to ensure that she respects their wishes. She also knows full well that Sprout may change their mind in the future and want to be known as "she." And she is aware that Sprout might just be too afraid to say. That's why she asks – to let Sprout know that she is listening and that they have her full support.

It's three years since Sprout opted to use "they," and they are still using it. It isn't some kind of phase. It isn't Sprout exploring their identity or trying to be one of their older mentors. It is who Sprout is, and Julie feels nothing but pride for them.

Spend the Money

At the time Sprout first announced their gender identity, Julie took them shopping with her. She went into a makeup store, and Sprout asked for mascara. Now, no kidding, Julie says her kid has superb eyelashes, the kind every woman wants. She's even thought, at times, how unfair it is that she didn't get eyelashes like that. Sprout already looks like they have mascara on – even when they don't.

When 8-year-old Sprout asked for mascara, Julie was a little torn. Even the 8-year-old girls at school didn't wear it! But, she says the staff at the makeup store were very supportive and appeared annoyed when she said no to Sprout until she explained that it was nothing to do with gender, only age.

However, Julie did start letting them buy makeup, or at least she bought it for them. But she noted that Sprout rarely touches it. Apart from a couple of experiments at home, they won't wear it in public and confessed to being scared of wearing it in the house should they be seen through the window.

But when they go shopping and head to a makeup store, and Sprout shows interest in a lip gloss, eyeshadow, or lipstick, she buys it, even though she knows it won't be touched. She buys it every time because, while it might seem like a waste of money, that bit of makeup means more than just makeup. It means she is supporting her child's identity.

When Sprout announced they wanted their ears pierced, Julie took them straight to a real piercer (no mall stand, a proper shop) because that is what Sprout wanted to affirm their identity.

Since then, Julie has lost count of how often Sprout has said how much they love having pierced ears because it's one way they can parade their identity. And yes, she does buy earrings she thinks they might like.

Whenever Sprout has a choice, they always go for the feminine one. But Julie says its money well spent if that is how they are comfortable representing their gender identity.

Get Your Child's Permission and Talk to Your School

Julie wants to be very clear about this – you must not go and talk to your school without talking to your child first. That's what this all comes down to – getting their permission. The first and most important rule in supporting a non-binary child is listening to them. Never do anything that could make them uncomfortable. They may not want the school to know, in which case, it's not your place to tell them.

On the other hand, they may want the school to know but are uncomfortable about speaking up. There is nothing wrong with that. Julie tries to teach Sprout to self-advocate, and when she has to go to school meetings, she takes them with her because Sprout must be involved and must learn to speak up for themselves.

However, talking to the school about your child's non-binary identity is different. Not all adults will understand, and some won't be supportive. Look at it this way – your child found it hard enough telling you; how stressful do you think it will be if they have to tell other adults, whether they trust them or not?

Sprout was happy that their mom was willing to go talk to the school, and after they had started using their gender-neutral pronouns, Julie headed off to talk to their teacher. Sure, the teacher didn't truly understand but tried to support Sprout as much as possible. When the new school year starts, Julie heads off to talk to the teachers in a private meeting. Sprout has made it clear that, in private conversations, even between themselves and a teacher, they prefer the "they" pronoun, but in public situations, they use "he." Yes, the teachers do find it hard, but Julie says it is worth the fight because it ensures Sprout knows they will all do what they can to make them comfortable.

What if Your Child Is Bullied?

Sadly this has happened to Sprout. Another child called them "a girl" in school, and it wasn't done nicely. Obviously, Sprout was a little upset, so they spoke to the principal. His response to the situation was, "people can like what they want." As far as non-binary kids go, that isn't a good response because it felt like the binary child was normalized, and the non-binary child was pushed aside as odd.

Luckily, Julie's school principal became more responsive, and when she expressed frustration, saying it could have been a good teaching moment by answering that not all kids feel the same way about their binary gender." The principal agreed and said a mistake had been made.

Even if your child doesn't want their gender identity made public, you can still support them by providing teachers with the right words to help the kids. A better response would have been something along the lines of "people should like what they want to like. Girls may like football, and boys might like makeup. We need to respect others because we don't know how they feel about their gender, so sensitivity is important when we speak." These things can be addressed by parents without "outing" their child in public.

Talk to Your Families

But only if you can. This is a tough situation. Julie's family is partly supportive and partly not interested. In fact, they haven't even told one set of grandparents because they aren't really interested in Sprout, and the conversation would be too tough. Sprout is already uncomfortable enough and, because the grandparents live so far away, they don't have much contact.

The other set of grandparents do see Sprout quite a lot but are stuck in a binary gender world. They accept Sprout's identity and mean well, but they won't use the correct pronouns. Julie talks to them, asks them to use the right ones, but they don't. And, in this case, Julie doesn't think it's a case of they won't. It's because binary genders are ingrained into their lives, and, sometimes, it's just too tough to change.

So far, Spout has said they aren't bothered because they love their grandparents and have never felt excluded. It's fair to say that these grandparents are even supportive of the earrings. In some ways, many ways really, actions really do speak far louder than words.

When It Is About You

We all know that this is about the kids, not about you, but sometimes it has to be about you. This is your journey as much as it's theirs. By supporting your non-binary child, you are on a unique journey of your own. Your journey may open you up to personal realizations and discoveries, and Julie has discovered that she is as good as non-binary herself.

Your non-binary child's journey is happening right alongside your journey. Yours is about being a parent, about realizing just how much you have impacted their sense of self and whether you have done the best you can. It has nothing to do with how everyone else sees your parenting and everything to do with how your child sees your parenting.

It becomes about you when your child suddenly hugs you and tells you they are thankful for your support, just because you stopped to buy them a pair of earrings you know they would like. Earrings that would help them express themselves in public.

It's about you doing everything you can for your child, and when you know that you did, you know that you did your best.

Let's go talk to Jo. They told their parents that they were non-binary and now feel a little rejected and confused.

CHAPTER 6

Jo's Story – What My Parents Thought

Jo is 14 years old. Six months ago, they announced to their parents that they were non-binary and bisexual. But they didn't do it in the normal way. Instead, they arranged a treasure hunt, ending in a closet with the bisexual pride flag proudly displayed. Jo's parents were happy that Jo had the confidence to come out and trusted them enough to share this side of them. They hugged them and told them that no matter what, they loved and supported them.

Jo says they haven't talked about it with their parents in the last six months, and they feel somewhat awkward trying to bring the subject up again. The problem is, they don't know who else to talk to. They did talk to their teachers and requested they use their chosen they/them pronouns – some are understanding but their English teacher lectured them about it and made them feel small. Jo didn't think their parents would want to know about this, so they didn't tell them. Jo has a lot of non-binary friends online, but they don't have any in the real world. With the pandemic still ongoing, much of Jo's schooling is online, and their parents are constantly on at them to stop using the internet so much. Jo is struggling with all the emotions they are keeping locked inside and they are starting to feel frustrated.

They really do love their parents and know that their love is returned, but Jo is starting to feel different, that perhaps they no longer have a place in the family. As time passes, Jo also feels that nobody truly understands what their life is about. Sometimes, it gets so overwhelming that Jo wishes their soul was in the right body, the body that everyone else sees as female. Sometimes, self-harming and causing pain to that body is the only way Jo can feel better and, when it gets too much, they even think about suicide.

Jo's parents are very worried. They can't understand how it got this far, and they don't know what to do about it. First, they have to understand what being non-binary means to Jo.

Jo doesn't feel they fit into the male or female gender. Some non-binary people feel like both. Some don't feel like either. Some also have very strong feelings that they don't have a gender.

Jo's parents need to understand that this is not a trend or a phase. Non-binary identities have been around for many thousands of years, but today's take on it is unique. In the old days, all identities could be understood within spirituality, but today's non-binary issues are discussed outside of spirituality and solely inside the LGBTIQ+ community. Some cultures even considered non-binary people to be wise, an embodiment of more than one energy, and were revered as offering a well-thought-out view of any situation.

Although Jo has come out as bisexual, their parents must understand that sexual orientation has nothing to do with gender identity. It's a bit more complicated than that. One of Jo's school friends told them that their friend announced they were non-binary but have stayed with their boyfriend, despite not being a woman. In that way, he was gender stereotyping his friend and assuming that sexual orientation and gender are closely related things. Even Jo knows that sexual orientation is all about who we are attracted to. Until we understand our own feelings, we have no right to predict someone's orientation based on what we see.

Jo's parents are also worried that they may transition, and that could mean expensive surgeries. It's a distinct possibility. For some non-binary people, it is the most important part of their journey. For others, it doesn't play a part. We cannot predict how anyone will feel about the body they were born with, and we certainly can't control how they feel. Much of Jo's dysphoria could be eliminated if their parents and friends truly saw them as who they are, not as a female or male. It is thought that dysphoria is a neurological difference between what a person feels and perceives.

Jo doesn't feel that they have a specific gender, and their dysphoria comes from confusion and from not being able to talk to their parents about their true feelings. They also feel that their announcement about being non-binary has been ignored. Over time, if this isn't addressed, this could become detrimental to Jo's health. They've already admitted to being tempted with suicide, and what's to say they won't do it one day? It's now really important that Jo's parents begin to see Jo as they are, accept them and support them and Jo needs their parents to know a few things.

Three Things All Parents Should Know

This doesn't just apply to Jo's parents, but to all parents of non-binary kids, especially those who ignore their child's announcement or just plan to refuse to talk about it.

1. *Self-harm is one of the most common mechanisms young non-binary people use to cope,* especially where they have no one to talk to. Non-binary kids are surrounded by people who don't understand what it means to not identify with a specific gender. In their eyes, non-binary kids don't know what they are talking about. They must be confused, not old enough to know what they want, or just going through a phase. Worst case, they are told to act like the sex they were born as. Being non-binary in a gender binary world is hard and overwhelming. If these kids don't feel like they live in an open environment, they struggle to get their feelings and needs across. More and more, they will bottle these feelings up until something breaks. Self-harm is often a way for these kids to feel alive. Jo's parents need to acknowledge their choices and show them they are loved and supported, which means using the correct pronouns as a start.

2. *Non-binary kids aren't broken.* If anything, it could be argued that society is broken for not including them. Commonly, non-binary kids have amazing people skills and a strong appreciation of others. They are more likely to make an effort to get to know people, to see past the outside, and look deep inside a person. Non-binary kids are not a problem that you need to fix. They have just as much, if not more, to offer as a gender binary kid, and, given a decent, healthy environment, they will thrive.

3. *It doesn't matter that you weren't prepared* – who is for that conversation? And sure, you'll make mistakes, but that's fine too, so long as you acknowledge them, correct the mistake and move on. The whole family is in this together, and Jo needs their parents' support. When a challenging situation arises, they need to ask Jo what their needs are. They could also ask themselves if they

46

need more information. Non-binary kids must be able to tell you their needs, but parents shouldn't seem like they are constantly leaning on the children, hoping their non-binary kid will help mom get through her feelings about things. This isn't about them. It's about Jo. Parents need to be responsible for their own feelings and needs, as do the kids, and the parents must ensure that their non-binary kid's needs are met at home and elsewhere.

Jo says they want their parents to get involved. They want to feel like their parents are listening and are comfortable with what they have to say. They want to know that their parents can deal with their feelings and doubts without making Jo take the blame. Jo finally feels alive. They feel like they can breathe, and having supportive parents is the most important thing to them. They don't expect their parents to accept it straight away, but they expect them to talk to them.

This was meant to be a time for Jo to celebrate who they really were, and it's meant to be a time for the parents to accept that they must change a little to give their child the room and opportunity to thrive happily.

Next, we're going to talk to Harry and Sarah, the parents of a child that announced they are a boy-girl.

CHAPTER 7

Harry and Sarah's Story – My Child Is a Boy-Girl

It's 7.00 am. It's a school day, and Harry and Sarah are both rushing to get their three kids ready for school. They need to be washed, dressed, fed, bags packed, and out the door in time, but then comes the spanner in the works. 6-year-old Jack rushes down the stairs crying his eyes out. Harry intervenes first, asking Jack what the matter is.

And so begins a journey neither parent even saw coming. A set of words they've never heard of and questions they didn't know they would ever have to ask. A note here – because of Jack's age, names have been changed to protect their identity.

Their new journey begins with a game. We've all played it at one point in time, and it's called "let's pretend." Jack explained that Yvonne, his little sister, wanted to play a game of "parents," insisting that she would be the mommy and Jack was the daddy. Jack protested that he didn't want to be the daddy, but Yvonne declared that he had to be the daddy as he was the boy.

Gulping back the tear, Jack said, "that didn't feel right to me because I'm a boy-girl."

Sarah has always prided herself on coping in any crisis, and, at that moment, she simply boxed the news away in her mind to be dealt with later. Turning to Jack, she gathered him up, saying, "whoever you are, we love you, so come here and give me a hug."

Harry felt as though he had reached the top of the world's largest rollercoaster. He knew that something was going to happen, but he didn't know what, and he didn't know what their journey would entail. All he knew was, this was happening for real.

Harry and Sarah had long known that Jack wasn't like other boys. He preferred female action figures to males. One day, he would be watching fairy movies and drawing dresses, and the next, he would be back to action movies, and all the stuff society expects from a boy.

Jack's parents didn't see anything wrong with this, and it wasn't an issue. Harry says there are many ways to be girl-like and just as many to be boy-like, but it was a little confusing at the back of their minds.

Sarah even started to count how many times Jack acted like a boy and how many times he acted like a girl. She did admit to being relieved when he acted more like a boy, though. Today, the day the news broke, Sarah noted that Jack was acting more girl-like, but he had been more boy-like for most of the last week, so she thought that would be how he was for the most part.

When Jack finally told them he was a boy-girl, she said it all started to make sense. But then she asked herself, "is a boy-girl even an option?"

Harry and Sarah had read plenty about transgender people but didn't actually know anyone who had transitioned. They weren't familiar with the term "non-binary," a term referring to people who don't feel as though they are male or female or who switch from one gender to the other and back. To Harry and Sarah, it seemed that Jack's status as a boy-girl could be the resolution they needed for all the years of confusion.

Harry says it just felt right, and three years on, he hasn't changed his attitude – it still feels right. However, this was just the beginning, and Jack's newly identified status was about to trigger a whole new set of worries that surfaced when Sarah was cuddling Jack before bedtime.

Jack asked his mom, "when you first realized I was a boy-girl, how did it make you feel?"

Sarah waited a moment and then told Jack that she was a little scared. All she ever wanted for any of her kids was for them to have a normal, safe life and for nothing to be hard for them to deal with. She said that she and Harry had known for some time that Jack's gender was a little different and swore that they would never make any of their kids fit the boxes society demanded of them. She did admit to being nervous because she wanted things to be easy for Jack.

Sarah turned the question around and asked Jack to tell her what it felt like to be a boy-girl.

Jack replied, "that's a hard question to answer. I don't feel any different from anyone else. I just feel like myself."

Sarah responded by asking Jack, "what about you is a boy?"

Jack got a little distressed and said there was nothing specific, that he just felt like a boy and a girl.

A few days later, Sarah tried again, asking Jack the same questions, but he ended the conversation saying it was too complicated.

That, right there, could be a summarization of their lives as they try to explain to their family and friends that Jack identifies as a boy-girl.

Finding Support from the Community

A couple of months after Jack had revealed his gender identification, Sarah took to Facebook to share it. She was looking for support, compassion, and maybe the answers to a few questions she had. She explained that she wanted to do it this way first, rather than face-to-face discussions, as she found it easier. First, she explained that her child was born a boy but now identifies as a boy-girl. She explains that, for the most part, they don't have a problem with this because they are a happy, secure family unit with fantastic friends who don't consider gender to be a barrier. However, sometimes they go places where no one knows them, and she gets asked quite a few questions. Sarah knows these questions come from the right place but often finds it hard to answer them.

"What will you do when Jack reaches puberty?"

"Isn't it your job to tell Jack who he is? You shouldn't be letting him work it out on his own."

So far, Sarah says the best piece of advice she has received is to let Jack lead the way, and that is exactly what the family is doing. She maintains that having control over a child is nothing more than an illusion that starts when you first see the ultrasound image of your unborn child. She and Harry started to imagine what their lives would be like with a son, imagining what he might grow up to be.

Clearly, that life is nothing like what they imagined, and to add to it, Jack is also on the autism spectrum. While Jack is doing just fine, his early years were spent with Harry and Sarah desperately trying to understand the diagnosis and help Jack cope with sensory overload. They also recently learned that autism appears to be higher among non-binary and transgender children but find it hard to understand how Jack's autism and gender identification overlap. Sarah and Harry both say the hardest thing right now is finding the right community for Jack, one where he is happy, relaxed, and feels at home.

They do take him to special needs camps and find they spend a great deal of time explaining non-binary to others. They also attend non-binary meetings, but the noise is often too much for Jack, and they have to leave before the meeting is over.

All Sarah wants is compassion.

She says she grew a person in her body who she thought was a boy. After being in labor for three days, she finally gave birth to Jack and asks those who seem to be struggling with Jack's gender to think about how she feels, wondering every day if her child will be okay when they are older. It upsets her when people raise objections against their decisions, and it hurts her too.

But with the best will in the world, both parents know that they will make mistakes, not just with Jack's gender, but personal pronouns too.

Speaking of gender, now things may become confusing, because we reach the point where Jack has asked to use specific pronouns.

Have Patience with Pronouns

Jack asked their parents not to use "he" as a pronoun anymore and use "they." This came around a month after Jack declared their gender identity, but some family members have struggled to comply. Jack's little sister, Yvonne, struggles, as do their grandparents, a few friends, and some of Jack's teachers.

Harry studies linguistics and says it isn't unusual for some people to struggle with a change in pronouns. "He" and "she" are deeply ingrained, especially older people, and we use them so much because it's all we have known. He explained to Jack that most people use "he," "she," "it," and "they" in just about every sentence they speak, and it will take a lot of practice and patience for them to get used to using pronouns differently. Harry said to Jack that it was much like walking. We are all taught to walk the same way but imagine if we had to learn a new way of walking all of a sudden. It would take most people quite a bit of time to get the hang of it.

Jack thought about that for a minute and then said, "like having to walk backward?"

Harry said, "yes, just like that."

Harry has to remind himself and those who saw Jack as a boy from birth that Jack no longer sees themselves that way and that they all have to get off that mental path now when they speak to and about Jack.

But his linguistics studies have taught him that, no matter how hard we try, how much we want something to happen, our brains are wired to talk in a specific way. As a way of helping, Jack has suggested that people refer to him as a group of people.

Sarah explained to Jack how his grandma remembers to use the right pronouns. She said that when grandma needs to remind herself, she thinks of God and, as she sees God as universal, neither her nor she but a "they," she thinks of God when she refers to Jack.

Jack's parents have been asked many times about referring to one person using "they," but they explain they have found numerous instances where language has changed to accommodate changing social customs. And Sarah was excited when she could show Jack a news story saying that "they" has been made the Merriam-Webster dictionary company's word of the year.

Jack was over the moon, understandably, but while it may be out of the norm for many people, many Generation Z and millennials are acquainted with using gender-neutral pronouns.

Clothing Codes

Jack loves wearing brightly colored clothes, in particular, those with animal pictures. Harry reckons that Jack wears dresses, boyish clothes, and gender-neutral clothes in equal proportions, roughly a third of the time each, and their curly blonde hair is down to about the middle of their neck.

Jack says that most people mistake them for a girl at first sight.

Sometimes, when someone makes the wrong assumption, Jack or one of their parents correct the person, but they don't do it all the time. They all agree that it would wear them out having to explain non-binary, boy-girl, or "they" to every person they meet, wherever they are.

Jack says they let it slide the first time or two because they understand it is new for everyone, and they don't blame them for getting it wrong.

The hardest thing for Harry was to drop Jack off at the school in a dress. He admits to being a bit squeamish inside about it at first but now admits it was only because it wasn't something he was used to doing.

His attitude has changed completely by watching Jack.

He says that Jack takes an awful lot of pride in how they look and when they are telling others. And Harry is so pleased that Jack's friends have taken to their new identity, like ducks to water, and is thankful they have open-minded families who don't pull their kids away from something different or new.

Using the Bathroom

Harry has lost count of how many times they've been told Jack is in the wrong bathroom – he says it has to be at least 50 – and most of them are kids at Jack's school. So now, Jack has a system for deciding which one to use. They use the men's or boy's bathroom on Monday, Thursday, and Friday, and the girl's or women's on Tuesday, Wednesday, and Saturday. On Sunday, they will use whichever one is on their right.

Sometimes, Jack's parents have to step in because, although Jack can choose which bathroom to use in Massachusetts, the laws are different depending on which state they are in.

Sarah remembers going on a family holiday to Hawaii and, because Jack was wearing a dress, they were told they couldn't use the men's room, even though there wasn't a queue. Jack did, and Sarah was upset, saying that although Jack had to go, she was scared they wouldn't be safe.

Jack was understandably confused, saying that he thought the laws had changed. You see, The family campaigned in Massachusetts for Question 3, which was passed, allowing Jack to choose the bathroom that fitted their gender identity. However, although it was passed in Massachusetts, they are unsure which of the other states have the same law. Jack could get into trouble by using the wrong bathroom or place themselves into trouble by entering a men's bathroom dressed as a woman.

Jack just said that all the people in Hawaii were nice, and they now know that Hawaii is one state where non-binary and transgender people are protected in public accommodations.

Future Preparations

Legal concerns aren't everything, and their parents have to think about that. Being Jewish, they have to start thinking about Jack's coming-of-age-ceremony. Hebrew is used for the ceremony, and there is no gender-neutral pronoun in the language. Jack has started planning a Bart-Mitzvah – a combination of the male bar mitzvah and the female bat mitzvah. But Sarah and Harry are concerned about how that looks because the ceremony is about affirming that you are a Jewish male or female.

As puberty approaches, Jack is set to define a brand new place for themselves in Judaism as puberty approaches. This is when Jack's voice will begin to deepen, and irreversible changes begin happening to their body. They have talked to Jack about it, and they understand that there are female and male bodies and Jack is comfortable being in a male body – that makes things a little easier because that's what Jack wants.

Harry and Sarah have sought some help for Jack through a Jewish program for LGBTIQ+ youth to ensure they are comfortable and can be who they choose to be. By the way, Jack has two sisters and calls themselves their "brister" – a mix of brother and sister.

Sarah is looking forward to getting help and guidance from those who understand life as a non-binary child fast heading towards teenage and adulthood. She says she has concerns about Jack's future. Even though Jack have affirmed their gender identity, and both parents have wholeheartedly accepted them, they worry about what happens when Jack reaches their adolescent years. They hope everything will be great for Jack, but who can tell?

Harry is confident that Jack will be just fine. He bases that on what he sees as a teacher, saying that his students are comfortable with there being more than the two binary genders. That says a great deal about the future, for Jack and their family, and everyone else. Harry is very hopeful that the world Jack grows up in will be one where they can be who and what they want without prejudice or fear of condemnation.

Sarah has heard a lot of people asking why, all of a sudden, all these kids are declaring themselves as non-binary or trans.

She says that Jack envisioned themselves to be the person they are. His parents never put obstacles in their way, but some kids will not have that luxury. However, it appears that more and more parents are starting to listen to their kids and support them in their choices.

Right now, Jack is involved in many things, from baking to building Lego projects, from a podcast about being non-binary to drawing their own comic book series. While they sometimes imagine these projects could lead to fame and fortune, they don't waste time dwelling on what the future will bring.

Jack says they will know their future when they live it. They don't want to waste time thinking about what the future brings because now is now, and they just want to enjoy life.

Phew! That was some story. Harry and Sarah are your role models here, the kind of parents every non-binary child needs and wants.

Let's about Roger, a non-binary teenager with some advice on what all parents should know about gender.

CHAPTER 8

Roger's Story – From a Teenage Point of View

If you met Roger walking down the road, you might struggle to determine if they were a boy or a girl. Roger is neither. Roger is non-binary.

Roger does not see themselves as being one of the two binary genders. They are convinced that there are multiple genders, of which their identified gender is non-binary. Roger has declared their pronouns as they/them, rather than he/him/his.

"Do you ever think about transgender people? Just a passing thought? You might have thought that this is something that a person becomes, but it's who I was born as. I've been this way forever."

As early as Roger can remember, society has tried to force the idea onto them that there are just two genders, that each one has its own specific colors, toys, clothes, and so on. As soon as Roger really understood that, they wanted to get away from normal expectations. They never wore a dress unless they were forced to. Instead, they wore leather jackets and jeans, trousers with their father's shorts, and had really short hair. They made their voice low and started doing things like drumming, skateboarding, and other typically masculine activities.

They believed it was nothing more than the activist inside them for a long time, firmly believing that gender should have nothing to do with specific colors and clothes. They had a deep yearning to break free of stereotypes, and that continued until they were twelve. They still believe that genders should never be given to inanimate objects, but Roger deeply believes there was another reason for their resistance. All they want to do now is help parents understand what being non-binary is like from the point of view of a teen.

How Roger Realized They Were Non-binary

It was sixth grade when Roger first realized that nobody has to identify as one of the binary genders. This was when one of their friends came out as non-binary, and Roger did a lot of research on the internet, learning that there were many different identities and, yes, non-binary was a real one.

When they looked at other people's experiences, they realized they were similar. They didn't feel right using female pronouns, and, before coming out, they found that she/her/hers were painful pronouns to hear. However, although he/

his/him felt better, they still didn't feel comfortable.

As a parent of a newly identified non-binary child, you might be wondering how such a small word can cause so much damage. These words don't have any real meaning, so how can they cause hurt to a person? Roger can't really explain it satisfactorily, but they do know that the misuse of pronouns hurts. It's just a feeling they have, and to Roger, that feeling is unquestionable. For example, Roger says if you identify as being male and someone refers to you as female, that might hurt, and it could possibly cause anger – the same applies to non-binary people too.

Your Child Was Scared When They Came Out to You

Roger found it completely terrifying to come out to their parents and, while they knew their immediate family would most likely accept it, it still took them nearly a year to find the courage to tell their parents. They heard too many stories of people getting kicked out of their homes after they had come out. Too many stories of families who denied their child's identity, trying to change them into what they thought they should be and, in some cases, trying to beat it into them physically. Roger was terrified that this would happen to them, even though they know, deep down, their fears were irrational. Thankfully, they say their parents have been completely accepting and supportive.

Roger has chosen not to come out at school yet. They know that too many people there still believe in only two genders, and they don't know anyone else who is non-binary or transgender. For that reason, they will wait until the time is right. They have found the hardest part is using the bathrooms – although Roger looks masculine, they have to use the female bathrooms, and people that don't know them stand and stare, whispering to their friends. To them, Roger seems strange.

Stop Misgendering Us

When you misgender a non-binary person, it's exactly what it sounds like — being referred to as a gender they are not. Roger lives in fear of this, so they wear their hair dead short, bind their chest, and try to be as much like a boy as possible. Being misgendered as a boy still hurts but nowhere near as much as being misgendered as a girl. They speak in a gravelly, low voice, wear their father's clothes, walk around in trousers, suspenders, blazers, and shirts, and when they catch sight of themselves in the mirror, they are happy.

The way Roger dresses, acts, speaks, just about everything they do, is to stop people from misgendering them, to stop people thinking they are a girl. There are so many things they want to do and so many things they want to wear that they cannot because people will simply misgender them.

You May Have Named Us But Call Us by Our Preferred Names

Roger says that one of the worst things you can do to a non-binary person is deadname them. That means calling them by the name they were given at birth. Many non-binary people change their names, preferring to be called by another that conforms to their identified gender.

To many non-binary people, their deadname represents the stereotypical box people have been trying to force them into since they were assigned a gender at birth. It represents the pain they feel of being misgendered, of people trying to force them to be something they are not. Not long after Roger came out to their parents, they changed their name. At first, it was hard for the family to remember the name, and it mattered so much to Roger that they tried hard. Their parents have now gone down the route of helping them legally change their name and updating their passport, even though Roger was terrified they would be against it. Their parents have done all they have requested of them and more. When Roger sees their new name on a plane ticket or a form, they are happy. It may seem simple, but the name change is significant – it tells them they are accepted and loved and can be who they really want to be.

The World Is Changing

And we all have a part to play.

As Roger was growing up, they always found society to be gendered. Clothing stores were typically divided between male and female, as are bathrooms. Most online forms require them to choose between male and female as a gender, neither of which applies to them.

This is changing, though. Take Animal Crossing, for example, a popular video game. The latest game released now doesn't offer a gender, only a choice of masculine or feminine-looking characters.

More and more websites are starting to offer different gender options, and even Roger's doctor's forms now have different choices. As a society, Roger would like to see nothing more than for us to advance, become more accepting, and eliminate the idea of there being just two genders. As a parent of a non-binary child, you can help by supporting your child, acknowledging that gender diversity does exist, and helping your child navigate an ever-changing landscape.

One day, non-binary pronouns will be universally accepted, and so, Roger hopes will non-binary people be.

Sound advice from a non-binary teenager, just a few of the most important things Roger says parents need to understand about their non-binary child.

In our penultimate chapter, we're going to talk to Susan, whose child taught her that gender is spectrum.

CHAPTER 9

Susan's Story – Gender Is on a Spectrum

Susan was sat in the car on the driveway when her oldest child informed her that gender was on a spectrum. Leslie had been at a youth weekend, and they were catching up with their mom. Susan turned to her 14-year-old and said, "No, it isn't. Sexuality is – you can be gay, straight, or many others, but gender is female or male, nothing more."

Leslie continued to insist that gender was also on a spectrum and wouldn't have it any other way.

Leslie came out as non-binary when high school was done, a bit of a surprise to Susan and Danny and a confusing one too. They both listened carefully to Leslie, saying they would be fully supportive, even though they had no clue what it all meant or where to even begin. Susan said if she pretended it would be easy, she would be lying to herself.

Up until Leslie was 18, Susan was convinced that her child was female until they announced that they weren't male or female and wanted their parents to start using they/them pronouns when they referred to Leslie in the third person.

As you have already found, in every chapter of this guide, pronouns are a critical part of a non-binary person's life and, while there are many to choose from, they/them are the most commonly used. Leslie now uses "they" rather than "she," "them" rather than "her," and "their" rather than "hers."

It's taken time and no small amount of practice, but Susan said she is now getting used to the changes, saying it might sound grammatically incorrect, but pronouns have deep implications.

Pronouns indicate the level of respect you give the person you are talking to. If someone says to Susan that they will continue to call Leslie "she" because that's what they are used to using, Susan feels they are judging her child by saying Leslie's comfort and choices are not important to them. She feels that they are saying that Leslie was born a female, and that's what they'll continue to call her because they don't understand or know any other way. Susan isn't sure whether they are being intentionally dismissive or they genuinely don't understand, but misgendering her child is wrong and hurts both Leslie and Susan.

Susan is aware that this might sound harsh, like she's requesting her friends and family, even strangers, to get involved in something that doesn't affect or involve them. She says that most of us know someone who is non-binary or transgender, even if we don't think we do – because how would you know unless they tell you?

Out of all the people she talks to, Susan finds that what she and her husband are experiencing is unique, but it's becoming more and more common each day. Leslie's mom feels she is doing all she can to ensure that her child and every other non-binary person can live in a world where they feel comfortable because that's what you do when you support someone you love. Susan has had long conversations with her parents, nearest friends, and even the cabbie and person at the supermarket checkout. When she meets someone she hasn't seen for a few months, and they ask how Leslie is, her reply is, "they're fine, thanks." When asked whether her kids are boys or girls, she says she has two boys and a non-binary child. Some understand and nod to show they get it, but mostly, she has to spend time explaining things.

Susan wants to share some of the questions she's been asked, and some of the reactions she gets when she talks about Leslie being non-binary.

"Do you think Leslie is just going through a phase?"

Susan constantly hears this question and her answer is always the same – no. Even if that were the case, why should it make a difference? The most important thing to Susan is to keep communication between her and Leslie wide open and to ensure Leslie is comfortable, no matter what. If she denies Leslie's choices, she closes that door and shuts Leslie out.

"That isn't possible! There are only two sexes, so there are only two genders. It isn't physically possible to be neither."

That really isn't a helpful observation. Susan isn't discussing sex. She talks about gender, a social construct that changes between cultures and from one era to another. Leslie told Susan that gender was on a spectrum, and the more she looks into it, the more she realizes Leslie is right. The only way Susan can explain it to others is this – most people see gender as male and female. Draw a line and put male at one end and female at the other. Lots of people, like Leslie, don't feel like the gender they were assigned at birth. Some move from one side of the spectrum to the other. Some feel like they are neither male or female and are somewhere in the middle. Yet others don't feel they are on the spectrum at all, and some feel their gender is not part of the binary gender system and call themselves non-binary. Those people will sometimes change their pronouns to they/them or one of the other sets of pronouns now commonly used.

"This is just Leslie trying to be unique, keep up with the latest fad. She'll grow out of it."

Just because most people who publicly came out as non-binary are younger than 25 doesn't mean older people don't recognize gender identity. They might not have needed to use the language or even know what it was, or they just might choose not to share it with others. We'll all find that non-binary is mainstream in a few years, and everyone will hear more of it.

"My kid said the same to me, but I think she's just depressed."

If you genuinely believe your child is depressed, get them the right help to deal with it. It may be that your child is down because you don't accept their identity, which is dangerous. Too many young people are driven away from family and friends or, worst case, to suicide because their identity is being denied. Do not do that to your child.

"I'm so sorry, it must be a terrible time for you."

No, it isn't, and I don't want pity – it isn't welcome, and it's most certainly misguided. The minute the thought goes through your head that you're glad it isn't your kid, you isolate those who identify as non-binary from the community. Keep your discomfort to yourself and respect other people's choices.

"You are so brave! I couldn't deal with that."

Again, this is terribly unhelpful and incredibly annoying, for all the same reasons as when people say they are sorry.

"Don't be ridiculous. You can't use "they" as a singular pronoun."

Delve into history, and you'll find language is constantly evolving – it's something you are going to have to deal with. Eventually, you'll get used to it.

You'll also find singular they in use since the 1600s.

"Couldn't you use "they" when you are alone and "she/hers" with the rest of us?"

No. Your child has chosen the pronouns they want you to use. Language is very important to them, and the only way to get used to it is to use those pronouns all the time. The more you hear those new pronouns, the more comfortable it will be to use them and the more welcome non-binary people feel in the community.

"I understand. The same conversation is happening in my house right now."

Get together and talk, share your experiences and frustrations – there will be some, not because you don't want your child to do this but because it will be hard for a while to get used to their new identity. Having a sounding board or someone with shared experiences is helpful and, the more there are of you, the more there are to advocate for non-binary rights.

"It's not that I don't believe you; I'm just confused."

There is nothing wrong with that – it's a lot to take in and get used to. You don't have to understand all at once; just promise to be open-minded and understanding. Promise that whenever you meet my child, you will be respectful of their identity and choices.

Susan loves her child. Leslie is the same sensitive, arty, active person they have always been. The only thing that has changed is their gender identity and pronouns. It's a learning curve for everyone, but it does get easier with time.

Susan has one last piece of advice – "accept it or don't but never disrespect my child or me by refusing to use their pronouns and not accepting their choices."

CONCLUSION

Most parents would do everything they could for their children. If your child falls ill, you seek medical help for them. If they want to do a specific activity or hobby, you do all you can to get them involved.

So, when your child tells you they are not the gender assigned to them at birth, what do you do? Parents face this question every day, as our children become more gender-diverse, a term we hear broadly used to describe a range of different gender identities, a range that includes non-binary.

Every family will support their non-binary child in different ways, and, sadly, some won't provide any support at all. Luckily, there are lots of ways you can support your child and plenty of resources you can use. One of the easiest ways to provide that support is to educate yourself on non-binary, gender fluidity, and gender identity.

What Does it Mean to be Non-binary?

When you educate yourself, don't forget to learn about gender diversity. Traditionally, gender was separated into two categories, and at birth, you would be assigned one of those categories, depending on your anatomy. Don't forget, we also have intersex people whose sex chromosomes don't conform to the stereotypical male or female. You have also learned that gender isn't one or the other; it is on a spectrum, and your reproductive system plays no part in determining it.

Transgender people have a different gender identity to the one assigned to them at birth, while a person who identifies with their assigned gender is known as cisgender. And then you have those that don't feel like they belong to the male or female gender, commonly known as bigender, agender, or non-binary.

Really, it doesn't matter where your child is on the gender spectrum. What is important is that you support their decision, support them, and make sure you use their preferred pronouns. Your child may choose to use the standard he/she pronouns, or they may choose to use non-binary pronouns, such as "they." It is their choice so ask, understand and use those pronouns.

It isn't a Phase

Let's be honest about this. You never expected your child to tell you they were non-binary. It was never on your radar. You may be surprised, but the most important thing you can do is to not dismiss their announcement as nothing more than a passing phase. The likelihood of your child just following the latest trend is extremely low, and, as parents, you must understand that you have to take this seriously and understand where your child is coming from.

The real key is understanding the difference between a child who isn't sure who they are yet and a child trying to communicate something deep and personal to you. The best way to understand this difference is to watch for messages from your child – insistent, consistent, and persistent messages. So, if your child regularly tells you they are not the gender they were assigned, you really need to listen to them.

And listen hard because they may not come right out and tell you. Other signs that they may not identify with their assigned gender could be in the clothing they choose to wear, conversations they have with their friends, or outright asking you to use specific pronouns.

As a parent, you may be wondering, "what if I accept them as they want to be, but they change their mind again later?" This is highly unlikely to happen. Research shows that most non-binary people knew when they were young and are not likely to change their minds now.

Supporting Your Non-binary Child

When your child comes out as non-binary, your first step is to tell them that you love them, no matter what. Sure, this may seem like a simple thing, but it is also one of the most important. When a non-binary child is given full support in their choices, their mental health fares much better in the long run.

You must tell your child that you accept them. Ask them to talk to you about being non-binary so you can find the right way to support them. When your child can freely tell you about realizing their gender identity, they share a personal journey with you that helps you better understand them. Don't ever think that your child being non-binary is an indication of bad parenting. It has nothing to do with that and everything to do with who your child is.

Don't be scared of seeking help elsewhere. Look for support groups, talk to your child's pediatrician or family doctor, trusted people who already have experience in raising or treating non-binary children.

Another way you can show your child that you fully accept them is to ask them how they think you can support them. What would they like you to do? Would they like for you to be there with them when they talk to the rest of the family? Do you need to talk to their school? Allow your child to guide you, to tell you what they need, so you can work out the best way to be there and support them.

I hope that you found this guide useful. Instead of dumping information, I felt it would be better to share personal stories with you. That way, not only do you get to learn the things you need to know, but you also get to see how other parents have handled the same situation and how the children themselves see things. At the end of the day, the most important person in all this is your child, and, provided you can give them your full support, the rest of it will naturally fall into place.

REFERENCES

August 15, Hank Pellissier |, and 2019 Print article. "'They' Is Here; Get Used to It." Parenting, www.greatschools.org/gk/articles/they-is-here-get-used-to-it/.

Forsey, Caroline. "Gender Neutral Pronouns: What They Are & How to Use Them." Hubspot.com, 2018, blog.hubspot.com/marketing/gender-neutral-pronouns.

GeekMom. "Supporting My Non-Binary Child in a Gender Binary World." GeekMom, 2 June 2019, geekmom.com/2019/06/supporting-my-non-binary-child-in-a-gender-binary-world/.

"Gender Pronouns: Importance and How to Be Inclusive." Www.medicalnewstoday.com, 12 Feb. 2021, www.medicalnewstoday.com/articles/gender-pronouns#summary.

Hardest Part of Parenting a Non-Binary Child Is Other People, Mother Says. www.pinknews.co.uk/2020/06/09/mother-hardest-part-non-binary-child-emotional-labor-dealing-other-people-new-york-times/.

"'I Just Feel like Myself': A Nonbinary Child and Their Family Explore Identity." Www.wbur.org, www.wbur.org/news/2021/04/01/nonbinary-gender-identity-children-massachusetts.

"I'm a Teen Who Is Nonbinary: Here's What I Wish Parents Would Know about Gender." Parents, www.parents.com/

parenting/better-parenting/teenagers/teen-talk/im-a-teen-who-is-nonbinary-heres-what-i-wish-parents-would-know-about-gender/.

"Is Your Child Transgender?" Right as Rain by UW Medicine, 10 Feb. 2020, rightasrain.uwmedicine.org/life/parenthood/transgender-nonbinary-youth.

May 1, Amber Leventry, and 2017. "I Was the Gay Kid, and Your Kid Might Be Too (so Practice Acceptance Starting Now)." Scary Mommy, 2 May 2017, www.scarymommy.com/parents-need-practice-acceptance-gay-kids/.

National Center for Transgender Equality. "Understanding Non-Binary People: How to Be Respectful and Supportive." National Center for Transgender Equality, 5 Oct. 2018, transequality.org/issues/resources/understanding-non-binary-people-how-to-be-respectful-and-supportive.

"Parenting and Supporting Your Non-Binary Child." Www.prideandjoyfoundation.com, www.prideandjoyfoundation.com/blog/parentingnonbinarychildren.

Reading, Wiley. "6 Ways to Support Your Non-Binary Child." Everyday Feminism, 11 Mar. 2015, everydayfeminism.com/2015/03/supporting-non-binary-child/.

Weiss, Suzannah. "9 Things People Get Wrong about Being Non-Binary." Teen Vogue, www.teenvogue.com/story/9-things-people-get-wrong-about-being-non-binary

CPSIA information can be obtained
at www.ICGtesting.com
Printed in the USA
BVHW010215110322
631231BV00014B/136

9 781087 979083